TAPESTRY IN TIME

As Seen Through the Eyes of a Poet

Carolyn J. Sibr

Fishermen's Inn, Elburn, Illinois

Cover Photograph by Marvin R. Young

STRAWBERRY PATCH PRESS
Clarendon Hills, Illinois

ISBN   978-0-6152-0876-3

Library of Congress Control Number: 2008903899

PRINTED IN THE UNITED STATES OF AMERICA

For my children Marnie and Frankie
as well as my grandchildren
Keira, McKinleigh, Kellan
Wyatt and Emma

ACKNOWLEDGMENTS

This book was possible because of the efforts of Paula Gossett who not only typed some of my manuscript but also has continuously motivated me with her optimistic attitude to write. I also appreciate the influence of Ed Searl, my minister, and Marvin Young, my good friend, who taught me the importance of living in the present. Many who have shared literary workshops with me have greatly contributed with their ideas and support concerning my poetry. Also, Heather Berg and Emily Hahn supplied assistance on computer techniques.

INTRODUCTION

The following poems are an expression of the wonder and awe found in the day's experiences.

Much happens to us as we travel toward our individual destinations, and we find the journey comprises the simple and ordinary expressions of daily rituals:

Cappuccino with a friend,
Trilogy of maroon trilliums in the forest,
Or the penguin-walk of a toddling child.

We enjoy the miracles of the mundane as we step from the past into the future with the concrete examples of twenty-four hours well-lived and appreciated.

Day awaits . . .
     opening the eyes
         of the morning glory,
     celebrating the vibrant grasses
         of the prairie,
     putting to bed the petals
         of the primrose.

Day awaits . . .
     its magic,
         a destiny
             of fulfillment.

The Fabric of Our Day

Seconds pass quickly,
    Turning pages
    of crimson cloth…
      an album of infancy.

Minutes tick resolutely,
    Counting down actions
    of purple passion…
      a journey of connections.

Hours beat softly,
    Moving steadily
    toward eternal daybreak…
      a river of destiny.
We step quietly,
    over streams
    beyond fences…

Into a sphere of transition,
    Transcending immediacy,
    walking into a world
of wonder,
  of awe, and
    of mystery.

We stand on a bridge
    of reflection…
We see
  trees,
    clouds,
      currents, and
        birds of paradise.

Our day ebbs and flows
    With tides of the moon, and
    warmth of the sun,
    With flux of fall, and
    sprouts of spring.

We clothe ourselves
    in vibrant colors
    of a changing world…
Our wardrobe,
    A fabric of our time.

SILK DAWN

Grandma's House

Flowers on glass shelves
Next to a window pane
Blue, white, and yellow

White, lacy curtains,
The fragrance of lemons

Sparkling early morning sunlight
On polished, cherry table top

Glass vase, pitcher and wine cache,
Dancing with rays of dawn

Ornate, Victorian buffet
Holding china dishes.

Charming

Fruited Air

God breathed early this morning-
Dull clouds precipitate
     into a singing rain,
Yellow daffodils dance
     under the maple tree,
Pregnant oak trees stretch
     toward a hidden cerulean sky,
Cheeky magnolias bloom
     with a purple blush,
Verdant lands sow
     into a virgin grass,
Napping tree buds yield
     into emerald leaves,
Dark blue squills ring
     with bell-like form,
White crocus clothe
     with satin dress,
Two mallard ducks bathe
     on the dappled lake.

God breathed early this morning-
The bluebell seeds sprout
     under the silent sun.

The Dawn

Vibrant…
        orange and yellow streak
across the sleepy sky.

Trees shiver,
Birds yawn,
Squirrels stretch.

Awake…
        the earth stirs-
no longer hiding under the covers.

Timeless

Past,
      but a vague memory,
           often forgotten.

Future,
      but a distant dream,
           often unattainable.

Present,
      but a priceless gift,
           always all that lingers…

           everlasting.

Marsh Musicians

From out of the hush
      of the reluctant aurora,
humming chatter penetrates the valley.

Trees pregnant with vitality
      listen for wind,
as tiny creatures hop for joy.

Grey clouds cover grassy knolls
      hiding spring's resurgence,
while swamps croak welcome to its visitors.

While winter warms,
      watching the return of the robin,
diminutive Peepers chirp their message:

    "From the stillness of the forest,
        burgeoning blossoms will soon
    resurrect the region."

Constellation

My shadow speaks
        in sunshine,
            moondust,
                and morning mist…

Not in
        cloudburst
        star break,
                or evening haze.

My shadow talks to me in all seasons
        Relentless,
Pursuing me
        as I walk
            through life's eternal sunlight.
A reminder of my soul's duality…

        My unicorn of daily experience.

Tryst

In a new day…

    the sun is warm,
    couples dance to Irving Berlin,
    the butterfly and bird fly free.

Thoughts let go of yesterday,
No concerns about tomorrow.

Today happens NOW

    With you

Beside me.

Dogma

The space is still and stiff with watchful Gothic pictures
and rigid pine pews. Even the blue of Mary's eyes and
cloak and the golden-brown hair of Jesus do not soften the
room's atmosphere. At the front of the church, the stern
pastor speaks admonishing the congregation for
inappropriate behavior. Standing with heads bowed, we
listen in trepidation and guilt. I am uncomfortable, not
apologetic, for attitudes that are inquisitive and tolerant in
relations to others. I glance toward the open window. A
breeze wafts freely across my face. The immaculate garden
outside beckons me, its natural state and beauty more
inviting that the Gospel. I can't wait to leave this building
and enjoy the temptations of the seductive Spring day.

Spring

The wind replants
    the seed
        of the flowering tree-

Chestnuts root
    Into wooded fortitude.

A River Runs Through It

The journey begins,
  a bubble of rain drops
   in the mountains,
   trickling toward the valley below.

They splash through
  meadows, prairies, and plains.
Past villages, towns, and cities.
over waterfalls and under bridges.

Surging into the sea,
they reveal a source of strength and wonder.
This rivulet runs within my soul,
washing through streams of self-consciousness.

They transcend time, space, and memories
  as their currents wash
   into an ocean of Self-awareness.

Siren Symphony

The lusty lake is my mistress.
Waters aglow in early morning sunbeams
Spread a golden radiant path to the skyline.

I await the day,
Eager to grasp the sparkling current
As she waves to my desirous dreams.

    She strokes me
as I walk upon her sandy beach.
    She plays with me
as I run my fingers through her rippled crown.
    Her depth seduces me
into ardent ambition.

Immense is her expanse,
so pure is her complexion.
She speaks in compelling crescendos,
a constant murmur of attraction.
I can't deny her presence,
    her beauty,
        her touch,
            her mystery.

How many have danced to her music
    and died in her rapturous arms?

Truth

The discerning dawn divulges
the spotted butterfly,
      Flitting from flower to flower.

The incessant insect,
      naked in the sun,
Gathers insight into the garden's composition,
      By drinking of its authentic wine.

Now

Where are the good times?
The poinsettia sits by the window
Watching grey overcast skies,
Flowers curling and
Dropping on the ground.
Left to dangle,
Three scarlet red petals remain,
Reaching toward the dim light.
 A brief reminder of past promise.

Where are the good times?

They cling to the moment

Dapple Grey

The sky blows Dapple Grey.
Not very much like clouds of May.
I see snow whiskered on winter ground
But my thoughts remember May's new dawn.

My minutes unfold in memory
Their purpose held so tenderly-
Take to task the moment of the day
As Spring presents itself in each slim ray.

Wilderness

This spring,
        So soft,
        A pastel peacock.
Arching over pathways,
        Still virgin
        To the human foot.

Far away from
        The concrete grove.
So far,
        The woods cannot be seen
        In the distance.

Trees, almost,
        In another place,
        Another time,
        Another world.

New Year's Story

A quiet time...
> to reflect by the hearth.

A tender time...
> to talk with friends.

A lovely day...
> Where the earth
stands still,
>> covered by snow.
> Where the rush of traffic
stops.
>> replaced by repose.

Champagne and
> good cheer left behind,
we ponder
> the nostalgic Christmas wish
coming true,
> of being with loved ones
just like you.

Peaceful Protest

The eagle screams at the sun's glare

while the dove hums

during daybreak.

A Moment

Morning sun
            Hot coffee
Cinnamon roll

Eyes open
            adjusting to the rosy dawn.

Breakfast begins
            early,
                a minute in the magic
            of the new day.

The Lodge
(From a legend told by Marvin Young)

We sit
>> languishing before a country breakfast,
>>>> eating heartily-
>>>>>> Staring at a rock,
>>>> where legend says
>>>>>> Indians once starved during warfare.

Once a native ground,
>> where a primal people gathered food
>>> and scavenged for peace.

Today a recreation area,
>> where many people go
>> to play and feast.

We watch
>> the drizzle dampen our day
>>> but not our hearts.

We look at
>> Glacier carved canyons,
>>> their islands now the home
>>> of the nested eagle.

We sit
>> looking at verdant trees spill.
>> down the deep gorge
>>>> to the rolling river.

We talk of
    climate change,
        illegal immigrants,
            and combat zones.

In the shadow of the bluff:

    Breaking morning brings,

        PEACE…

Faith

Sun shines

within me

even on the cloudiest day.

Hope

On a
visit
to my home,
my granddaughter
spent hours
playing
hide and seek
with a
cardboard box
when she
was
two years old.

A child recreates today's divine destination.

The Morning Meadow

The meadow,
       a community of grass and insects,
Nestles by a stream with a solitary tree.
A spectacle of flowers
       illuminate a colorful corsage
on a breast of clover that covers the ground.

Deer frequent the blooming plain,
       feeding on native strawberries.
Quiet,
Nothing hears the distant bulldozers,
far enough away
       from civilization's asphalt drive.

A Christmas Carol

The delicate trees are alive with song
as they dance to the dazzling tune
of the snow syncopating on their limbs.

> White diamond flakes dangle
> in arches brushing the arbor in
> glistening dew, silencing the sky
> with soft pillows of pearly velvet.

The path winds through the sparkling scene
unmarked by any traffic
but my own footsteps.

> I stop to hear the sound of a stream
> gurgling over a dam. The only
> creature I see is a red cardinal
> in a crabapple tree.

After a morning of hectic holiday shopping,
I find peace and prosperity in this
winter winsome woodland.

Bargain Price

Morning embrace,

Woodpecker's melody,

Fruited meadow,

Star-kissed sky…

Are nature's bonus,

They are free!

As the World Spins Around

Winter winds whistle
Across the battered landscape.
Bold. Biting. Boisterous.

They encompass the pain of illness
       And death;
But life continues day by day,
As the scarlet cardinal rests
On my friend's spruce tree daily
Despite the turbulence of seasonal angst.

Pool of Serenity

A pond surrounded by woods
       Down a secluded lane,
Scurries with life,
       Yet is still a peaceful place.
Green frogs and brown rabbits hide
       In twisted grasses from strangers
Invading their home.
       Slimy snakes slither
Into the thicket,
       Showing their fear of intruders.
Weeping willows drip
       Into the grey-green waters,
Shading the sandy soul.
       Birds trill
In tree tops,
       Warning of foreign footsteps.

The pond,
       A spot we seek
To ease life's burdens,
       And find silken repose in Nature's nourishment.

Creation

In the beginning,
A Great Big Bang...

    To fill a void with embryonic matter,
spheres of scraps and residue,
and boundless galaxies and stars.

    A combustion of fire so great,
atoms formed...
Planets to whirl around these heavenly
beams in conjunction with moons and comets
to pursue infinity.
Great oceans developed fish, plants,
animals, and finally humans
to populate the luminous earth
and take care of paradise.

Was this God's Grand Design or
        Celestial Chemistry?

The Madrigal

His eyes touch me,
hopeful as the pledge of cherry blossoms.
he laughs at my awkwardness,
smiling like dew at dawns dither.
he walks at my side
a shadow of destiny.
he converses quietly about the days magic,
spinning stories of my desires.
he seeks companionship,
breathing air into my struggling lungs.
he remains silent,
only to be heard by the harp of my heart.
he has been called
messiah…
    son…
        brother…
            teacher…
                friend…
                    traitor…
he comforts me,
leading me to merciful lands,
where the sun falls beyond the horizon.
he sleeps peacefully beside me,
only rising again to morning's melody.

Destiny

We lie not in the finite grave,
But in the breath of eternal Spring
As the morning mist dances on the daffodil.

20/20

Do I react
      with fear
            to the obscure night?

Or do I respond
      to the sun's inherent light?

Like the rooster's crow,
      I awake
            to dawn's discerning might.

TAFFETA NOON

Sanctification

Ceremony of sapphire skies
and emerald grasses
with an altar of marble
 and open doors

Ceremony of everywhere
near and far

We stand by fountains of flowers
and pews of pine;
we congregate with many

Around us we hear
hymns of the earth
songs universal

A golden chalice of fire illuminates our Vows
the genesis of "our Promising New Life;"
we unite Together Side by Side

Summer Solstice

Purple posies shed
their green satin skin.
Buds flourish,
Opening an umbrella of radiant blush.
Inside the petals,
Fragrant foliage enraptures air,
Introducing bees with sweet ambrosia.
Dainty flowers flow to a peaceful breeze.
Stems bend softly,
Whistling in a pixie wind.
The woods flourish in self-esteem.

Tea for Three

I'd prefer to see a splashing waterfall
Than a high-rise building.
I'd prefer to hear the crunch of fall leaves
Than clattering machines.
I'd prefer to smell a savory lilac
Than palatable perfume.
I'd rather ask "Why?"
Instead of say "Amen!"
I'd prefer to notice a moonbeam
Than a neon light.
I'd prefer to touch a raindrop
Than a satin dress.
I'd prefer to share a cup of tea with my friends
Than anything else.

Hospitality

Love welcomes a stranger
So the maverick comes home to his family—
His body embraced by their greeting,
While a wine goblet toasts the homecoming.
So the voyager discovers his treasure—
His hand holds an album,
While he pictures his personal endearments.
Love reaches beyond our doorstep
Our neighborhood unites with the rainbow's hue—
Refracted rays brighten stormy skies,
By reaching out to a bruised companion—
The homeless, the lonely, the broken...
Love caters to community
Empathy's ethnic celebration lures seductively—
Room for one more

Granddaughter

She appears
with golden hair
brown eyes and rosy cheeks
the princess
then turns
to smile
at her audience

Listen

Listen…
the spoken word not heard.
conversation disappears into the hush of an iron cell,
conventional clichés halt the sound of a heart beat,
insight twists silently into an emotional pretzel.

Echo…
Answers with a sound.
Hearing a word,
It repeats your intent—
Becoming a voiceless image,
Parroting a narcissistic dialogue.

Listen…
Not a noise uttered.
Anger muffles compatibility,
Partners efface empathy.
Quiet reigns—
Hear the pin drop…

Treasure Chest

The sky burns greenish blue
Clouds drift pearl pink
Leaves flutter ruby red

Winds bluster
blowing falling foliage
to the ground,
Leaving taffeta trees
highlighting the horizon.

The view visible for many miles
promises hope
for fall's redeeming rudiments.

Alice

She appears old
as wrinkles puff across her high bony cheeks.
Her snow white hair twists straight back
into a ring of silk at the nape of her neck.
She is thin,
so thin she appears emaciated
from time spent in a concentration camp.

Yet, she rises from her chair easily, anxious to get to the
podium where she will speak of long ago romance: palaces,
beaded gowns, princesses, and fairy tales. Her musical voice
sings of fantasy and folly. Her eyes blue and as deep as a
Caribbean sea rivet our attention. In her eyes, we picture a
child with red pony tails telling of imaginary places. As she
weaves her story creating a land of wondrous adventure, we
realize youth is in your heart!

Freedom Trail

Footprints unfold
in crunchy white snow
They wind
toward the sunlight,
a golden globe of destiny.
Steps of desire…
they mark the grove,
showing determined self-reliance.
Footprints emboss
the winter wilderness,
a mark of distinction.
They lead
toward a path
of insatiate independence.
Their road bedazzles accomplishment.

Real Estate

Winding roads weave
through spacious, opulent timber.
Acres of land unharness
man's technology of homage.
Wild flowers bare their breasts
against untouched, untamed grasses.
Forest reaches
to touch the sky,
independent from suburbia's shackles.
Calculating man asks:
"How can empty land have value?"
Suddenly a redwing blackbird flies
from amongst the brush,
searching for his mate...
Precious

Prodigy

A walk through the meadow reveals
that the wild strawberry is a miracle.
Crimson,
Beneath the sun,
It's an ornament of summer sensation.
It sparkles with dew drops,
after rain showers moisture
on its berry.
White flowers parade
to the orgasm of a rainbow's tinct.
Pearly petals prepare
for another day
as they beacon to the butterfly.
The plant rests quietly
with undisturbed grasses,
and reminds me in their silence—
Life,
like the lush fruit,
Is a treasure-trove.

The Garden of Eden

The monkey…gregarious…
swinging from a tree limb…
does not complain about his plight,

The giraffe…lofty…
graceful in gallop…
does not whine about his sins,

The lion…courageous…
stalking his prey…
does not worry about his prosperity.

They live in their natural habitat…
self-composed…
strong in their will to survive
not seeking God's benevolence.

So I visit the zoo—
To be with the animals and their innocence.

Enchanted Woods

The day is apple crisp. Leaves crunch at my feet as I walk
through amber swells of forest. Scarlet umbra splashes against
sapphire skies. I hesitate -- the call of birdsong is gone. But the
squirrels still play in the brush hoarding seeds for their winter
stash. The meadow smells of burnt nostalgia, the fragrant
garden limp and fervent from the cold night air. The water on
the pond, no longer still, waves to me with ripples blowing in
the gruff wind. My mood is optimistic since I can imagine the
legacy of the season as one of reaping as well as one of sowing.
I shiver when I face the chill of autumn, so I stroll to my car
looking forward to a bowl of hot, warm pumpkin soup.

Suburban Renewal

The prairie grass so smooth
It melts into a field,
But hides from concrete slabs
Made to be neighbors' homes.

Velvet land so meager
It needs to be cared for
Or daisies from the pad
Will not find room to grow.

Tenants belong by sod
For winds to stroke their face,
Birds sing their songs of love-
Leave space for nested doves.

Spontaneous Combustion

Like
    golden leaves unravel in fall
        and purple violets spiral in spring,

Life
    just happens
        with you.

Christmas '07

Snow warms
　　the earth
with the brightness
　　of the season's
good wishes.

The red cardinal rests
　　on a green wreath
of pure joy.

A stream rings
　　over a dam
chiming
　　for a pool of peace.

The forest ripples
　　in silence
as deer prance
　　in solitude.

A woman walks
　　cautiously,
so not to disturb
　　a world white
with fertile serenity.

Two- Way Street

We share…

    casual clothes

        scenic drives

            folk music

                endless conversation

                    workshops

                        poetry readings.

Yes, we meet…

    unpretentiously,

        as you accept me,

            with my red crocs and blue jeans.

Mentor

He stands above us,
Yet is our peer.
He speaks of dreams
        that unite us,
Not of dogma
        that divides us.

Through him,
        we hear of cardinal wings,
        Albert Schweitzer, and
        the day's divinity.

He does not preach,
But teaches of...
        mountain streams,
        holocausts,
        justice, love, and compassion.

We experience his counsel
as he ministers to our spiritual growth.

He answers to Reverend;
We call him Ed.

Pandora's Box

Sometimes

    it is enough

to just dream

    rather

than pursue imagination.

Livin' Easy

I use to walk a path
      where wild strawberries grew
among the fields.

With the sultry sun beaming
      upon lush red berries
I would hike and explore
      with friends.

Those summer days have faded,
      but red berries and white flowers remain
in the open grasses of the forest.

Among the scratchy thistles,
      echoes of those days still whisper
as I walk today
      through perennial strawberries
of my youth.

Winter Carol in the Forest '07

We are intruders...
    Snowdrops drift
        upon tree limbs,
    leaving white lace
        on fragile branches --
pearly ghosts of winter present.

    Snowdrops fly
        in the wind,
    floating to the ground --
        ivory angels of winter's harvest.

    Snowdrops collect
        on the lake,
    crusting at the water's edge --
        bright diamonds of winter's treasure.

    Snowdrops dance
        on the prairie grass,
    floating across a frosty field --
        sequined ballerinas of winter's nutcracker.

    Snowdrops glimmer
        in easy silence,
    creating a harmonic interlude --
        cryptal cupids of winter's melody.

We are discordant intruders...
        crushing these silver snowdrops,
            melodious instruments of peace.

Joy

nothing
sounds so sweet
as
wind chimes
softly
chanting
from
the limbs
of a maple tree

Faith

Down
the winding road,
there is a
white church
bronzed by
honey sun,
with a
belfry
that rings
every noon
sounding softly
through the
brisk breeze
of an
autumn afternoon.

Experience reinforces our belief systems.

Sometimes

Often, it's so satisfying
To glimpse summer rain
Sprinkle sparkling jewels
On red rose petals...

Have a date
      With dewy dawn...

Hear the thunder's cymbals...
Often, it's so satisfying!

Then, you come home
To the dirty laundry
And appreciate nature's magic even more.

Kaleidoscope

Velvet green of innocence,
Colored with…
       purple passion and heliotrope honesty,
Captured on yellowed paper-
       an album of memories.

'Tis the Season

Far from the forest swings
      an evergreen wreath.

With red ribbon and
      snow-crusted pine cones,
it rests outside my door
      on a black iron patio fence.

It looks foreign
      in these surroundings
as it is commingled
      with brick walls and
          asphalt driveways…

No longer do cardinals and
      squirrels nest
in its branches.

No longer does it twist
      in the wind
          of sun-drenched air or hear
      the staccato of a chattering stream.

It is now placed
      in the shadows of society.

Where cars drive
      by in a hurry and
mostly ignore its beauty.

Yet, it braves neglect
      by blowing proudly
in a breeze of esteem.

Offering simplicity and genuineness
        to some residents
                of a complex, commercial condo:

The wreath hangs
        with the humility of hope
that its worth be realized.

The Chapel

The church has . . .
    no cross,
        no bells, or
            steeple.

    no wine,
        no grapejuice, or
            bread.

    no dogma,
        no organ, or
            Bible.

Still,
    Congregants come,
        to celebrate the Divine . . .
      the mystery of the universe,
      the undying day,
        the sanctity of nature, and
           the dignity of people.

SATIN SUNSET

Cozy Comforts

When leaves ripen
    and reveal brilliant colors,
I like to drive to the country
    near a smooth, flowing stream
Where ducks swim in gentle waters.

Strolling with my favorite friends,
We visit a village inn
Nestling next to the race's edge.

    Here, we converse
    and pledge allegiance to our souls-
    a handshake of the heart.

We sip tea from simple ceramic cups
    and eat pumpkin pie.
When days are bright and brisk.

Journey

The road

     to the mountain top

   is often

      very rocky.

Rainbow Years

Long ago:

     puberty awakened innocent awareness

     school gave rise to inspiration

     a diploma promised new horizons

     cars traveled to destinies unknown

     part-time jobs established self-respect

     minimum wage provided rich reward

     friendships sparked generosity

     a kiss aroused tenderness.

Long ago,
     when raindrops resonate into a spectrum of color.

Birthday Quest

Outside,
    Sunshine dimples
on the water's rippling current.
    Ducks and their brood huddle
in misty shade,
    avoiding humid heat.
    Children stroll down the winding river walk,
as canoes drift upstream.
    Flower bouquets float
Like in a garden of joyous gems.

Inside,
    a birthday cake decorates a rustic room,
commemorating an album of passing years.
    Dripping candles celebrate
a long life of rebirth.

A silent wish responds
    to the celebrating guests' song:

"May many years result
    in a heart
        that beats with springtime
    of each coming year."

Evergreen

Fireflies dim in the night,
    their flicker no longer beats
    to summer evening's two-step.

Crickets cease to sing
    an overture to hot nights
    of celestial slumber.

Cooler breezes brush
    through trees
    as mute mums droop
    in the crisp morning air.

The sky seems bluer,
    like an azure sea,
    as it prepares to shift
    to waves of wind-blown clouds
    streaked with charcoal grey.

Green forests begin
    to be tinged
    in a subtle golden hue.

Nostalgic memories of summer disappear
    as the vibrant season dips
    into the dusk
    of tomorrow's transitional days:

A time of harvest and of seeds of resurrection,
    when fall reaps the final reward-
    the sowing of the summer spruce.

Migration

In this season of changing colors...

Geese,
with excited and raucous voices,
fly with wings unfolded
across chilly skies of blueberry cream.

Vagabonds,
they seek new homes of milk and honey.

Winter Solstice

Day grows dim,
        sparked only
by the incandescent falling snow,

A reminder of evenings past,
        when candles softened
the dark rays of winter dusk.

Cold nights passed easily then…
        cold toes warmed by white wool socks,
        grilled sandwiches toasted with cheese,
        a monopoly board covered by play money.

Peace prevails inside our fortress,
        the fireplace sizzles and
        popcorn snaps.

Howling winds do not chill
        our winter rose.

The Pearl

Day is but
       a second
In the hour of infinity…

It endures
       as the bright sun falls
beyond the scarlet terrace…
       a legend of our fragile fancies.

Live it well…
       as day's opal omnipotence
redeems renaissance.

Until We Meet Again

We sat in the car,
looking out the window…
        not touching

We talked about the day,
glancing into each other's eyes…
        not touching

We said goodbye,
kissing…
        a touch until your return

Twilight

A room

      black with obscurity

waits for another day.

Then a sudden glow

      of breaking morning

shines through the shaded windowpane.

Recycling

Snowflakes...
    white
        bold
            beautiful
                unique.

Nature's mandala...
    Showing the planet's cycle of...
    life
        death
            rebirth.

The wholeness of moving molecules
individualized by the interdependence of
the explosive and expanding cosmos...
    energy
        dirt
            gasses.

Frozen crystals melt into the soil,
only to transform and evaporate again
into the clouds, and become the source
of spring rains and...
    the rebirth of the flowers.

Expectations

I once sought the sophisticated world,
To travel far in anticipation of tomorrow
But now I view the simple earth close at hand
In the enjoyment of today.

Once I ran swiftly
Down stony paths toward sunset,
Now I walk slowly
Upon brick blocks toward dawn.

Once I gossiped loudly
On the telephone,
Now I chat softly
Over a cup of tea.

I once journeyed
Toward distant shores,
Now I am content to navigate
Toward ports called home.

My Friend Karen

A golden cloud halos her face.
Her eyes fresh as morning mist
     glance into my soul.
Fragile as a daisy's breath
Strong as a winter's wind,
     She faces her demise...
         death
     with calm serenity.

Her life an angel's flight,
     she reaches toward the zodiac
making each day a sacred journey
     into the present.
Her aeon becomes a diamond on Olympus-
     an evergreen moment in the immortal flight
         of the universe.

Redemption

I threw a rock
        into the resting river and
watched the ripples race
        beyond the reclamation.

How little
        it takes
                to impact
                        the environment.

All the Time in the World
(Dedicated to the Virginia Tech Massacre)

Youth,
        Students...
Planning for the future,
Caught in the present:
        Classes
                Homework
                        Friends
                                Lovers
                                        Graduation.

Then, a crescendo of despair:
        Gun Shots
                Frightened Screams
                        Ebbing Blood
                                Anguished Death.

The hour stands still for some,
        No longer to be touched
                by the dawn of day:
                        Tears
                                Grief
                                        Condolence
                                          Memorials.

Minutes tick toward sunset,
Only to reveal Sirius...
        Etched in golden rays.

Recollections

Far away,
    In the distant past,
Thoughts breathe
    In the recesses of desire.

Now,
    All but dreams,
Their magic proves divine.
    Recalling a melody
    Recalling a face...
Requires de'ja vu.

    The good old days,
Never seemed quite so good
Until they became a memory.

The Embrace

The caress,
for an instant in infinity,
we held each other close --

Our arms,
entwined with tenderness,
the impassioned silence
       pervading our very core --

We stood together,
for an instant in time,
caught by surprise --

       the caress
       the affection
       the silence
       the wonder

And you and I perceived…
       for everything there is a season.

Fall

The peacock of the seasons.
Showy.
A reminder to plant an acorn for tomorrow.

Street Person

Concrete, high-rise barriers encourage shadows.
Weeds break through sidewalks.
People corralled by buildings.

An isolated man sits on a doorstep,
His eyes dulled by whiskey.
He rests on factory steps,
Waiting for a scrap of food.

Blocks away, the Gold Coast,
Where affluence wraps itself in nonchalance.
They turn away from poverty,
Strangers to leftovers.

The addict's eyes haunt the street,
Walled in by the city's compulsions.
Alone,
Against the seedless street.

Yesterday

Once upon a time --

  Children played in a meadow
and saw birds nested in an apple tree.

  There were strawberries
to be picked,
streams to fish in,
snowmen to be built --

Once upon a time.

Today's Moment

I returned to the valley
Today,
To my home,
Now abandoned by me.
I lust for its river bed,
Its emerald wood,
Its golden corn fields,
Its tart apple cider.

I walked in the sun
Today,
Surrounded by fall's gaiety.
I wound around the river's edge.
I came home to my vintage mums
With a friend beside me,
To feed the ducks
And taste the tea's sweetness.

‘

Valentine

I'll never forget
      that minute
the moment you looked at me,
      and smiled.

That smile
      so tender
it carried me home,
      to gentle times,
where things were simple and secure.

So secure,
      I did not sense,
the wind and wrath of winter.

I'll never forget
      that minute
the moment you took me home,
      to your home,
now our home,
      where space is soft and sweet.

The Silvery Choir

Silence is nature's melody
Of good intentions-
      Its harmony of prayer.

The Geisha

Voluptuous,
      A bud of beauty.

Demure,
      A promise of ecstasy.

Eyes,
      A gift of allurement.

Body,
      A cocoon of mystery.

Temptress,
      A sultry dancer...
smiling subtly,
          NOW.

Stuff

Teddy,
Once beautiful,
soft and huggable.
Now, a worn bald bear:
his bountiful body
limp and shabby...
magic still in his beaded eyes.

My daughter's favorite toy cuddles in the closet,
A keepsake to be loved by her children.

A Time for Wine and Walnuts

Spring of pink blossoms and
summer of painted flowers evaporate
from my view.

Robust leaves rush to earth,
pushed by a lusty wind.

The season matures intensely...
    magical mums bristle
        in still morning air,
    plump pumpkins grin
        from pruned fields.

Frost nibbles at my feet
    as I walk down the path
        of my spicy journey...
        days of consummate community,
        nights of virginal valleys.

I feel the cold breeze,
    see the grey sky,
        touch the salty soul,
            taste the tamed temperament.

I am no longer spry,
    sassy, or
        self-sufficient.

But I still find peace:
    luxurious morning glories,
        gaggling geese,
            sweet apple cider,
                poetry of a gilded pond.

Now the days rest early,
Darkness comes quickly.

Golden embers of today's flame light
    the hearth of winter's glowing fire.

Evening Primrose

Nightfall reaches out to us,
    holding us close . . .

        We dine on popcorn,
            we watch Venus, and
                we listen to Simon and Garfunkel.

But most of all,
    we talk about . . .
        day's enduring dream
           of an infinite spring.

VELVET NIGHT

In the Beginning

Obscurity shrouds the night,
Enticing the owl to hoot,
    the child to slumber,
        the moon to shine.

Night,
    a charade
Encourages illusive dreams,
    images questioning our desires.

Dark,
    often seen as evil,
Soothes the stars
    as they radiate
    in constellations of stellar candescence.

With night,
    came light…
    a sun to warm
        earthly life and vision.

At night,
    we restore our creative strength,
So as to ripen
    in dawn of day.

Benevolent night,
    invisible…
        immeasurable…
            inevitable.

Moonglow
(inspired by John Mahoney)

The rose,
　　　silver in moonlit nights,
inspires starbright imagination.

The crystal garden
　　　splashes with clear goblets
of honey sweet nectar
　　　resting on lily-white leaves.

The rose,
　　　swaying softly with a subtle breeze
suggests a gentle feeling
　　　of dazzling delight.

Auld Lang Syne

hands held together by the hearth of hope

tender mercies in the night

dinner for two by the candlelight

walks along the lake

conversations of intimacy

eyes warm with tenderness

My glass toasts our days
      of tea and empathy...
   our days
      of sugar and spice...

A year of comfort and joy!

Yesterday's Song

A melody sings through the seasons-
   a rush of gentle wind
swirling to the measure
   of memories metronome...
      the spring of a planted seed,
        the summer of a blissful union,
          the fall of a thankful harvest,
            the winter of the womb's creativity.

Memory beats in our veins
flowing through generations,
   a gift from the Heavens,
touching the heart
   of our human experience.

We remember the waltz of time
   as we dance
to the tune of today,

Knowing that we are enriched,
   by this epoch resonance
of the past.

The Glowworm

Fireflies flit across the evening sky-
Their lanterns of light illuminate the dim eye.
Like stars at night,
        They search the infinite gloam...
Searching for the divine Gnome.

Dialogue with Death

I am the great equalitarian-
all are welcome through my doors.

I am the siren that sings
all through one's life
and no one may escape my song.

A crystal ball
seldom predicts my arrival.
I am feared by most and
greeted by some.

I bring transition to all;
I am the fall that colors
the leaves before they drop to the ground.

I am an enigma-
no one knows if I am an end
or a beginning.

I reach out to you in your dream
and when you are awake.

I am your constant companion,
your friend, and your perennial pendulum
into the expanding Cosmos.

Epithet

Minstrel of breathless wind
alone,
answerable to no one
only myself,
embraced by the universe
baptized by raging waters...

a mistress of insanity
loved by the Sun
I am a child of Jupiter
mother of the Moon
and,
companion of Mary Magdalene...

Heaven

We fall asleep,
        only to return
                home…
Our place of
             destiny
with the stars.

Socrates

He appeared in my dreams...
        mentor, teacher, and soulmate.

Talking of rainbows,
        we shared the seasons...
                lilacs, roses, and mums.

We hiked mountains...
        walking, running, and climbing.

Side by side,
        we conquered...
                pride, prejudice, and paranoia.

With him
        the day emerged...
                immediate, hopeful, and fulfilling.

There were no empty moments,
        no wasted minutes;
                but an hourglass
                        of infinite galaxies.

Sirius Street

Brilliant star-
  shining
   among the constellations

Sweet murmurs
in the night,
tantalizes softly
with its radiance

A wishing well
of profound passion,
a volcanic interior
kissed by fire

Evening star-
  so close
   yet so far,
    pursued by the Magi

A highway to the heavens.

Milky Way

Stars swing
       through the sky,
Dancing eons
       of kinetic, explosive energy.

They dangle overhead --
       magic in their movement,
An encyclopedia of evolutionary design.

Death and rebirth alter their constellations-
A subconscious pathway to today,
       as they burst from our submerged past
       into our volcanic present.

They have been our omnipotent Gods,
       and our infallible demons.
We have worshipped in their luminous light --
       Goddesses of Homeric harvest
       and Pierian spring.
We have cringed in their elusive eclipse --
       Gods of celestial wars
       and cultural infertility.

We question their mystic origin,
       and their absolute power.

Like comets,
       stardust conceives our genes.
Like stars,
       our initial journey travels towards forever.

Nightfall

Bold --
The sundown settles
hiding pure pink, delicate clouds.
The restless whirls
of night
devour
the enchanted sunset.
The licorice sky
awaits
the taste of dawn.

New Beginning

The silver moon slid silently
     across the solemn sky,
Striking a shimmering ball of light
     against the midnight shadows.

Bells did not ring.
Horns did not sound.
Champagne did not flow.

The New Year came softly, slowly…
     with a friend at my side,
     a song in my heart.

Katrina

She came silently and slowly. As silent as
salmons swimming upstream.

Stealthy,
She washed ashore,
Covering all asleep in the asphalt night.
Nothing was spared. As waters rose,
people and animals scrambled onto
rooftops waiting for the comet hope
of dawn.

The flooded city wreaked a harvest
of death, decay, and destruction.
A Mardi Gras of confusion paraded
the streets trumpeting an SOS for
survival and resurrection.

A paralyzed nation watched and waited
and finally responded to the submerged
hostages of the angry hurricane.

Evacuated,
everyone awaits the final word on
the future of a town's destiny.

Everything has a new beginning --
But where, when, and how?

Heaven

Are we the heirs of God's infinity?

With a dove's wings,
        hope abounds the skies
and the clouds dim with sunlit serenity.

The morning glory awakens
        the dawn of purpose,
giving a plan to hazy fall days.

A drop of rain fuels
        the grace of salty seas,
providing will to surging waves.

A tiny seed becomes
        a faithful fruit tree,
feeding birds of prey.

An iridescent rainbow encompasses
        a peaceful earth,
calming angry waters and wind.

As a crocus revives in spring,
so do we inherit the love and beauty
of today's treasure chest.

Why?

The world's fragrance wafts into enigma:

        dawn breaks open,
        springing across red rose buds
Morning begins in mystery...

        baby's first cry,
        embarking into new life
Morning begins in mystery...

        Monarch butterflies migrate south,
        rising from their cocoon of hope
Noon begins in mystery...

        constellations consolidate stars,
        illuminating earthly breath
Night begins in mystery...

        white crosses drip over the dead,
        resting amongst aching meadows
Night begins in mystery...

        heavens hosts the trinity,
        affirming love and peace
Night begins in mystery...

Our planet migrates around the sun,
        its nosegay of creation an enigma...

        Day ends in mystery.

The Compass

South
    Grandfather Sun…
Lighting our day,
Promising hope for fertile soil and
fruitful vision.

East
    Father sky…
Embracing heavens,
Expanding the stars of the cosmos.

North
    Grandmother Moon…
cradling posteriority in candlelight,
cleansing the tides of time.

West
    Mother Earth…
Breathing into the lungs of plant and animal life,
Birthing the womb of nurturing sustenance.

The Globe…
    A magnet for interdependent cohesion,
      a family of creation.

The Candle

Rosy wax
      drips
into the crystal bowl.

    Melting,
Measuring our time together.

Chat Rooms

I shared my dreams with you, Nestor,
        Fantasies of the night --
They were not dark illusions,
        But castles in the sky
Where a white stallion carried us
        across the harvest moon.

I was at your side
        as you swept me beside you
in a carriage of silver stardust.

We laughed together,
        we cried together…
             about everything,
             about nothing.
        we talked of…
             sunset firecrackers
             dancing dew-lit mornings
             the isolation of Ishmael
             breaking bread with nature
             the breath of community.

The day sprang from the heavens.
It was time to go --
        My shiny moment with you ended.

I walk into the stark sunshine of social uniformity
        where my computer's cold aloof communion
with my peers diminish my identity, stimulated
by our alluring presence with each other --
        the music of our tranquil tangency.

Shine On!

To some the moon means madness.
Others see its magic.

But to me,
The moon reflects mystery.

Resting Place

While walking in the snow,
I watched it melt into the ground
And felt the pang of spring's surrender.

        Innocent flakes
        Floated through the air,
        Landing on blades of grass,
        And then were swallowed by the soil.

How ironical.
After a long, significant journey
The spangled crystals were abruptly cradled into the earth,
Just like I will be.

A Prayer to the Planet
(after a Mohawk prayer)

Thankfulness to Mother Earth,
      bridesmaid of the night and sky...
and to her seeds: unique, fertile, and fragrant
      in our thoughts -- let it be.

Thankfulness to Wild Life,
      our kin, friends, teachers...
showing ways of freedom and self-reliance
giving of their meat, brave and cunning
      in our thoughts -- let it be.

Thankfulness to Water,
      clouds, rains, rivers, and icecaps...
including or delivering; flowing toward
all our briny tides.
      in our thoughts -- let it be.

Thankfulness to Air,
      the song of soaring Eagle wings...
singing the Swift stanza of Daylight
a fresh breath of Spirit breeze
      in our thoughts -- let it be.

Thankfulness to Sky,
      whose infinite expanse holds boundless stars
it is beyond us and in us-
Grandfather Time.
The Mother of Invention.
      in our thoughts -- let it be.